Beverly Adkins

Transcending Life-Course Events
Through

A

Patchwork

Of

Love

© 2011 Beverly Adkins. All rights reserved.

ISBN 978-1-257-96957-9

Acknowledgments

I am indebted to my sister, Barbara, for her literary skill and inspiration, as well as to God for every provision.

Table of Contents

Preface

Introduction

She Knew Water

Now By This I Know

What Manner of Man is This?

A Patchwork of Love

Preface

Age old Bible stories are presented here to provide a fresh look at some issues that prevail today. *She Knew Water* characterizes the desperate need of a disenfranchised woman to fill the void in her life. She is a social outcast who has not found a meaningful love relationship. More than that, Jesus has to demonstrate to his followers that the Gift of Life is for all humankind.

In *Now By This I Know*, a life-giving miracle is rendered to one who has only heard about the true God, who has already lost her husband, and may lose her son. Finally, those who are privileged to walk with the Savor of Life unto Life experience a life threatening event that forces them to exclaim w*hat manner of Man is this?*

The craft of quilting is suggested as an analogy to the restoration that God has designed for each and every one who is drawn to the Living water, as we come to the realization that by His love we can know Him, as well as witness the power of a Man not seen in any other.

Introduction

For centuries, Americans have used pieces of cloth and worn clothing to weave quilts into functional and creative memories. Numerous patterns provided warmth and beauty in a social learning environment that paved the way for once-traditional roles for women.

A special kind of ingenuity and resourcefulness adorned beds and showcased quilts along walls as a reflection of pride and self-esteem.

Quilts were even used on back porches and along fences to guide weary travelers (e.g., slaves) in search of a new life. Uses, notwithstanding, quilting events provided social interactions that welded families and communities together. Thus, the craft of quilt-making makes an excellent analogy as to how God restores lives that are tattered by sin.

The work of Creation, needless to say, was no piece-together job. There was already a plan designed to patch together this sinful world. The following stories exemplify how assurance in restoration is provided to anyone who pleads for *living* water, for the soul of another, or for one's own soul salvation.

"She Knew Water"
(John 4: 1-42)

Some of us are unsuccessful at love. But, because we are created social beings, we long for it. One woman failed at love for more than just a few times, so much so that the search for love had become frustrating. Lacking a lasting and fulfilling relationship, she was reduced to settle for a love of convenience. It was to visit such a one as she that Jesus had come to Samaria.

The trip had been long. Peter, who was always a step ahead of the rest, lingered behind.

He was still puzzled over Nicodemus' late night visit. "James," Peter beckoned from the rear. "What did you make of Nicodemus?"

"What do you mean, Peter?" Peter drew closer to James to keep the others from hearing.

"That business of being born again. What do you think He meant?"

"Well, James reflected, "it wasn't about our natural birth, obviously."

"Obviously."

"So, it must be a different kind of birth…a spiritual birth, don't you think?"

"Of course," confirmed Peter.

"I'll ask the Master to explain further."

"No, no," Peter said quickly, "that won't be necessary." Peter was too proud to admit that he did not fully understand the Master's words. He only hoped to figure it out for himself.

Judas seemed withdrawn from everyone on the trip. Peter surmised that Judas was deeply absorbed in all that Jesus had taught. However, that was not the case. 'Why this traveling back and forth?' Judas wondered. 'Surely, I can set up a forum to get Jesus to power more quickly. Then, I can have the position I deserve next to Him.' Devising a way to come between Jesus and John had, also, become a consuming pastime for Judas.

Once in the city if Sychar, Jesus sat down at what was known as Jacob's Well. He had become weary of travel and just as weary of His companions. He knew that they had yet to understand who He was and what He had to teach them. Would they be able to grasp the important lesson just ahead?

"Master, wait here," Andrew suggested, seeing that Jesus had already stopped to rest. "We'll go to town for food." Such was Andrew's portion – always accommodating.

Alone, Jesus felt the extent of His fatigue and thirst. He ached. He knew that He could collect water to quench His thirst. He could summon angels to wipe His brow, but He chose not to. Instead, He suffered the bands of humanity and waited for the divine appointment.

It was about midday when she came to draw water. She was an attractive woman, though her ill-fitting clothes assaulted her frame with every movement. Always she had come to the well to quench her thirst – or maybe her loneliness – and always she felt thirst again. She gazed at the well as if in a trance. Her lips parted but, for a long time, no sound was heard. There were many things in her life that did not satisfy. Now, she was troubled that her beauty was fading and that life was passing her by.

The well had become her solace. She could talk to it and it would listen. It even humored her to think that the well answered her when the glistening water trickled into her bucket. That was all the response she needed. Each day, she told the well how she identified with the water trapped inside it, and how she was envious of its many visitors. No one ever came to visit her, so the pain of a love dying from neglect was all she had come to feel.

Then, a gentle voice spoke, "Give me a drink." She had been oblivious of the One already waiting there. She stared at Him in unbelief.

"What? Aren't you a Jew? And, You ask me, a Samaritan, for a drink?" She had hoped to dismiss Him and get on with her misery, not realizing that she had grown comfortable with it.

Looking at her heart, Jesus knew her pain. It would have been easier to have drawn the water Himself and have it waiting for her, but that would have made her suspicious of His gift. He had to reach beyond her hurt to draw her closer. In asking her for water, He had hoped to give her something greater. He continued, "If you had known the free gift of God, and who it is asking you for a gift, you would have asked of Him and He would have given you *living* water."

"You don't have a bucket to draw with," she announced. She knew this well, and she knew its water. She had come to this very spot every day at the same time. She knew how many steps it took to get there, when the water was cool, when it was warm, when the well was crowded, and how much water and how long it took to fill her bucket. *She knew water!*

At this juncture, she could have walked away. But, being curious about many things, she asked, "Where do you get this *living* water?" Then, an attempt was made to divert the conversation from the purpose of their meeting, but Jesus continued to explain what He knew about *living* water (i.e., a wellspring unto eternal life, from which no one could ever thirst again). He had her rapt attention.

"Sir, give me this water, so I won't have to thirst, nor come here again."

He replied, "Go, get your husband and bring him back with you."

Her pain, momentarily forgotten, jolted her body. Living with a man to whom she was not married had its own kind of degradation. She felt wretched. Looking to the ground, she answered, "I have no husband." Again, she wanted him gone, but her sin had to be revealed to her.

"You have been married to five men, and the man you are living with now is not your husband. You have spoken the truth in saying that you have no husband," Jesus rebuked her ever so gently. She was amazed. His demeanor was most comforting. Yet, once again, she sought to divert their discussion from the purpose of their meeting. It was when her conversation shifted to the coming of the Messiah that Jesus informed her, "I am He."

Meanwhile, the disciples, on returning with

provisions from the city, were surprised at the familiarity between their Master and the woman. They stood silent, waiting for an explanation. But, Jesus would not enter into any controversy with them. It would be one of many lessons lost to them.

Immediately, the woman dropped her bucket and ran back to the city. She found a group of men there and entreated them saying, "Come, see a Man who told me all things that I ever did. Could this be the Christ?" They followed her back to the well, some already believing and some only curious.

Now, the disciples could not understand why Jesus would not eat, nor could they grasp the lessons He drew from nature and from her harvest. The Sent of God explained, "My food is to do the will of My Father." The men of Samaria urged Jesus to stay a few days longer that they might hear His words. And, in due time, many more came to believe on Him, saying, "Now we believe, not because of what you said," looking at the woman, "but because we have heard for ourselves and know that this is, indeed, Christ, the Savior of the world."

Gladden by these words, Jesus' heart was full. This was the food His disciples failed to understand. Prophets of old had foretold of the coming Christ. Others would recognize the divinity of His voice and in His touch. The Father had already acknowledged Him as His Son at His baptism. And, now, the despised of Samaria were given to this revelation. Peter, the first in many things, would proclaim the Lordship of Jesus Christ. But, that was yet to come, not until the five thousand were fed. Dull in understanding and still unacquainted with the Savior, those privileged to walk with Jesus would remain strangers to the divine influence. The lessons would have to be taught again. For now, she, who knew water, had come to know the Light of the World as the One called *Living* Water.

Heart

"Now By This I Know"
(1 King 17)

It is a terrible thing to lose your husband. The tragedy in losing someone so dear is in losing half of yourself, as well. So it is today, and so it was in ancient times. A widow loses her husband and soon learns that it is impossible to live in his reflection. She tries desperately to hang on to his memory but the smell of his skin, the lines in his face, even the way he enters a room, soon fade away. Add to that a famine in the land and a son to raise, and you have a picture of the widow of Zarephath.

She was troubled much by the loss of her husband. For some time, there had been long periods of empty disconnected feelings. Then, there were jolts of reality, reminding her that he was, indeed, gone – him kindling the fire each morning, while she kneaded bread; the odd jobs that did not get done around the house; and, crawling into bed at night and not finding him there. Today, a new day in her grief, she would have to collect wood for the fire herself. Her agony, then, would be the only thing to hold the memory of her husband close to her.

At the gate a voice was heard, "Please bring me a drink of water." At first glance, she could tell that he was not from Zarephath, nor from the surrounding cities of Tyre and Sidon. Clad in humble garb, the visitor's outer cloak signified a special office. He was a prophet. Her feeling of uselessness was quickly abated as she turned to get the water. Then, more than simple hospitality was added to the request, "Also, bring bread with you."

Turning back, she answered him saying, "As the Lord *your* God lives…" (perhaps a previous visitor had already introduced her to the true God of heaven in that pagan wasteland) "I don't have any bread, only a handful of flour and a little oil. And just now, as you can see I'm collecting wood to cook the last meal for my son and me, before we die."

A sickening feeling came over her. For the first time that day, she had thought of her son.

How different it was before her husband died: the three of them always together.

The man of God answered, "Fear not. Do what I have asked you to do, except feed me first. And, afterward, cook for yourself and your son. For this is what the True Witness says: 'the bin of flour will not be used up, nor will the jar of oil run dry, not until the Lord sends rain upon the earth.'"

It had been Elijah, himself, who had

pronounced the famine that cursed the land. And what was the famine like? Empty cisterns, a parched ground, nothing to plow, animals giving birth and walking away for lack of grass, others sniffing the wind like wild jackals (Jer:14) – such was their portion. Notwithstanding, Elijah was confident that God, who had provided water at the brook of Cherith and the ravens to feed him, would surely continue to sustain him. Had He not said, 'I have commanded a widow at Zarephath to provide for you?'

As for the widow, the thought of eating her last meal to join her husband in death was appealing. The emptiness had been more than she could bear. Why not give up her last meal to the prophet? She had stopped liking the taste of food some time ago. So, she went and did according to what the prophet had told her. Much to her astonishment, she, Elijah (as she had come to know him), and her son ate for many days, thereafter. The flour was not used up nor did the oil run dry, just as the Lord had spoken.

Elijah continued to reside with the widow and witnessed to her about the mercy and power of God. Just having someone with whom to talk brought new energy and life to the widow's home and heart. Temporal and spiritual sustenance was provided and, with renewed strength and faith, the widow took up living again.

"Now it happened after these things," the record reads, "that the son of the woman who owned the house became sick...so serious that there was no breath left in him." How easy it is to overlook the little ones. The loss of her husband was so great, that having a son who remained was not much comfort to her, nor was she much comfort to him. She was looking for the day when she could look at him and not be reminded of her husband, but that day had not come. She was overjoyed that, with the visitor, came food to eat. However, she failed to notice what toll the famine and the loss of a father had taken on her son's frail body.

In a panic, she questioned why the prophet had visited her. Was it because of her sins? The alternative of sending her son through the fire to appease the god of Baal had no appeal to her, not even to save her husband from death. Had she not loved her son? And, now, while enjoying what little comfort that had evaded her for so long, she had allowed her son to slip always. Death was to slap her in the face a second time.

'It was the God of Elijah who had done this,' she reasoned. 'Would He, like Baal, have to be appeased? Was He any better?' Her faith had not been complete.

"Give me your son," said Elijah. He lifted the boy in his arms and carried him to his room. There, Elijah touched the child's lifeless body and, convinced of his own weakness without the power of God, he pleaded with the Lord in the child's behalf. "O Lord my God, why have you brought tragedy upon this widow? Let this child's soul come back to him." Meanwhile, the widow's inaudible sorrow had not failed to reach the throne of heaven.

Hearing the voice of Elijah, "the soul of the child came back to him and he revived." Elijah returned the son to his mother and, with a loud voice, he exclaimed, "He lives!"

It felt good to have her son again, to touch him, to love him, to hug him. *"Now by this I know*," the widow affirmed, "you are the man of God, and the word of the Lord in your mouth is the truth." She no longer spoke of the Lord as the God of Elijah. In complete faith, He had become her God, as well.

What Manner of Man is This?

(Mark 4: 35-41)

Both physical and mental exhaustion occur when we constantly experience feelings of being tired and worn out. Causes of this phenomenon can be attributed to excessive stress from myriad changes in the living environment (e.g., sleeping deprivation, eating problems). Hormones are released in our bodies to help us cope with these stressors. However, when chronic stress reaches a point where the body is unable to adjust, serious consequences are inevitable. If left unchecked, exhaustion can lead to the boil-over effect (commonly referred to as burn-out), depression, or a lower functioning of the body's immune system. It was from this kind of physiological deterioration that Jesus was experiencing when He said, "Let us cross over to the other side."

His day had been full of activity. Many parables were shared with the crowd in attendance. He explained that the kingdom of heaven was analogous to wheat and tares growing side by side until the day of harvest (Matt. 13: 24-30); the growth of a tree from a tiny mustard seed (Matt. 13:31-32); and, leaven hidden in three measures of meal (Matt. 13:33). He, further, explained that the kingdom of heaven could, also, be equated to hidden treasure or a beautiful, expensive pearl (Matt. 13:44-46); a fisherman's net that gathers fish of every kind in one catch before they are sorted (Matt. 13:44-48); and, the way in which a householder labors with old and new possessions (Matt. 13:52). Had His listeners understood that, in nature, the wheat and tares meant that people are not always what they appear to be, that all professing Him would not be truly transformed; that the gospel would spread even from the planting of the smallest seed; and, that the value of salvation was worth a great treasure and something to be sought after? Rendering practical examples of what the kingdom of heaven is like and distinguishing outcomes for the good and the bad had been exhausting work. Thus, going to the other side meant crossing Gennesaret, a fresh water lake fed by the Jordan River, lesser streams, and other underground springs. Even today, it provides irrigation for the areas that surround it, some good fishing, as it continues to attract visitors.

In ancient times, however this same body of water was Chinnereth as referenced in Old Testament Scripture (e.g., Deut. 3:17, Josh. 19:35). Jesus had called His disciples to become fishers of men and healed all manner of sickness along these waters. This was where He fed the multitude with the two fish and five loaves of bread. And, although much of His ministry had taken place in this area, He was now tired and hungry. Surely, the other side of the lake would provide Him with the needed respite away from the pressing crowd, so that a new lesson could be learned.

Reclining at the rear of the boat, Jesus fell into a peaceful sleep. It was the kind of sleep that escapes many of us. Daily concerns linger in our minds and are, often, carried over to the next day. We go to bed with our minds troubled by unfinished business. What develops is a list of things that we need to do. We think about what's been said, left unsaid, and things we have no control over, but wish we did. At bedtime, muscles tense up and impede the next day's activities. No wonder that sleep disorders are prevalent! At the very least, some of us try to re-train our minds to mentally focus on "pleasant" images so that mental journeys can take us to other places. Still, sleep therapies require effort, but Jesus' rest was not in therapeutic images. His rest was in the knowledge of His Father.

Suddenly and without warning, the sky grew dark. Gale-force winds shrieked through the mountain gorges, typical for the area. There had always been a two-fold destructive/constructive process that sculptured the sharp edges, crevices, and gorges of Lake Gennesaret. This storm, however, was more intense as the resulting tempest blew horizontally across the boats on the water. Tremendous pounding from the wind and water increased the pitch and roll dramatically. Water filled the vessels and the ride became rough and frightful. The disciples grew faint as it became too dark to see the angry blast that howled in their ears. Soaking wet, the skill these men had as seamen was of no avail. The boat was sinking and, through it all, Jesus slept undisturbed.

Aware of imminent danger, fear gripped the disciples. It was not the usual kind of fear that makes us anxious about disease or loss of health. Nor was it the kind of fear we have of losing face when our pride has been injured. This fear was more pervasive because, as human beings, we become attached to this physical world and, when that attachment is threatened, we fear the loss of life. We become insecure, lose faith in our worldly significance, and fear that mortal harm will befall us.

For the disciples, it was the here and now. Both mind and body had worked in tandem to generate stress. There had been a distortion of time and perception. Everything was moving in slow motion. There was no black and white, just black...pitch black. Blood pressures elevated. They had tunnel vision, but not that which causes error in judgment. They were everything they had practiced to be. Except for a few, at least four of the disciples were seamen first. Simon, Andrew, and brothers, John and James, had practiced the skill of navigating the waters. Still, they failed.

Feeling overwhelmed, every attention was directed at what was truly valuable to them. Past arguments, self-centeredness, and position posturing seemed petty now. 'Perhaps, I should have been more tolerant," were the thoughts that flashed through their minds, but only for a second. Fear had returned. There was no easy way out. The boat was filling with water. They could not shut down to pursue different alternatives. No time to be indecisive, no time for confusion. Every effort was bent on keeping the boat from capsizing. Perceptions were not clouded as everyone looked to the leadership of the fishermen on board. These had been courageous men who were completely preoccupied with saving themselves.

Now useless and full of despair, the disciples began to accept their fate. They were going to die just because they wanted to cross the lake. But, why were they on the lake? Then, they remembered at whose biding they had set sail. In their panic, they had forgotten about Jesus and did not know where He was. Someone called out. Then, another. There was no sound or sight of

Him. Perhaps, He had fallen overboard. It was not until a flash of lightening broke through the darkness that Christ was discovered sound asleep amidst all the turmoil. Everyone shouted in desperation, "Master!" and He awoke. They could not imagine His, seemingly, lack of concern for their circumstances. How could He sleep when their lives were in danger?

"Don't you care that we are about to die?" were the words heard above the storm. But, when they saw how calm He was, they relaxed enough to plead, "Please save us."

No plea for help would go unheeded. Jesus stood up and raised his hands. It was the posture that the men had seen many times when He healed the sick and when He spoke to the crowds that pressed against Him. There is something about the way we carry ourselves (e.g., our gait, the inflection in our voices) which is how we are known. Jesus, often, raised His hands the same way. Speaking to the wind and the sea, He said, "Peace, be still." The wind stopped raging and the sea settled. As quickly as the storm began, all was tranquil. Nothing was disturbed. Turning to the men, Jesus questioned their fear, "where is your faith?" Experiencing a different kind of confusion, they looked at each other for answers: *"What manner of Man is this?"*

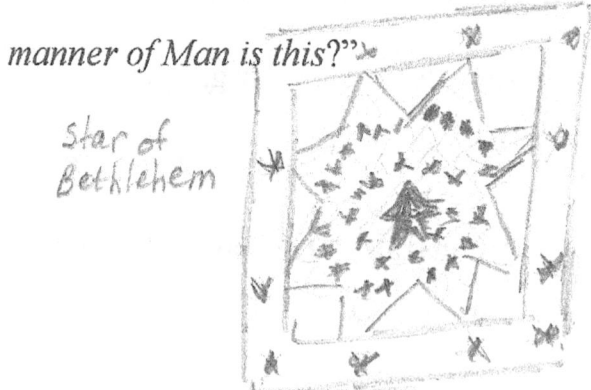

Star of Bethlehem

A Patchwork of Love

Genesis 1

Barbara Drake and Beverly Adkins

We know the Creation story: How the Spirit of God moved over an earth without form and spoke into existence all that was made and said that it was very good. Carrying out *their* purpose, man was formed and, later, woman to live in obeisance to God. Christ communed with the garden couple, so it is not surprising that God has always desired to commune with us. But, something happened to that relationship.

Partaking of the forbidden fruit, the first couple's eyes were opened and innocence was lost. Sin began to take its course to ravish and unravel the lives of all born in this world. So, how can a thread-bear world be restored? There was a plan.

In close communion with the Father, Christ made supplication. He offered to give His life as a ransom to take the sentence of death upon Himself. The Design was to rectify a disastrous state of affairs and present God as He truly is. Humanity would see His true character shown in Christ to restore the lost image. It would be a *patchwork of love*. So, "when the fullness of the time was come, God sent forth his son, made of a woman, made under the law to redeem..." Galatians 4:4, 5. Thus, it became our privilege to see how the divine plan should look and to know that "he which had begun a good work in us will perform it until the day of Jesus Christ" (Phil. 1:6)... "the author and finisher of our faith" (Heb. 12:2).

Using the analogy of a quilt, every thread, every stitch, cross-stitch, and seam is inevitably related to the Great Pattern. Silently, the Divine Quilter reached into His kit and pulled out the needle of faith and the thread of hope. Like so long ago in the shade of Jacob's Well, He stitched the wounded soul of the wayward woman back together. Just as the double stitch is used to stabilize and embellish a fragile design, what Christ did laid the groundwork for subsequent relationships to build on. To wit, there is no chaotic situation (e.g, the loss of a husband, impending death of a son, wailing winds) that God cannot remake into something good. He did it at Creation, at Jacob's Well, the Gate of Zarephath, on the waters of Gennesaret, on the cross, and He continues to do it today.

www.ingramcontent.com/pod-product-compliance
Lightning Source LLC
Chambersburg PA
CBHW061511040426
42450CB00008B/1562